CRYSTAL CLEAR

How to Use the Earth's Magic Energy to
Vitalize Your Body, Mind, and Spirit

BY CONNIE CHURCH

Illustrations by Penelope Gottlieb

VILLARD BOOKS NEW YORK 1987

Library of Congress Cataloging-in-Publication Data

Church, Connie, 1955–
Crystal clear.

1. Quartz crystals—Miscellanea.   2. Occultism.
I. Title.
BF1442.Q35C48   1987   133   87-40225
ISBN 0-394-75642-8 (pbk.)

BOOK DESIGN BY GUENET ABRAHAM

Manufactured in the United States of America

9 8 7 6 5 4 3 2

First edition

THIS BOOK IS DEDICATED TO

The light
The truth
And the intrinsic good that exists in all of us

ACKNOWLEDGMENTS

First, my deep appreciation to my teachers for sharing their knowledge and their guidance: gifted metaphysician and psychic astrologer Gerald Jackson of Charlotte, North Carolina, who has taught me so much about life, the laws of the universe, and who consulted on this book; Linda Waldron of New York City, who first introduced me to the power and magic of crystals; and crystal healer and metaphysical psychologist Zoe Artemis of Los Angeles and New York City, who has guided me to a new understanding of myself. Zoe also contributed some of the material for Chapter Four—especially on the chakra system.

As always, *eternal* appreciation and thanks to my wonderful literary agent and close friend Al Lowman, Authors and Artists Group.

A *special* thanks to my editor, Diane Reverand, with whom it is always inspiring to work.

Also, thanks to Allison Acker for her editorial assistance, to Brian Moore for his special assistance in helping me "take good care of business," and to Emily Bestler for her support and her attention to the little details.

My gratitude to Penelope Gottlieb for her magical illustrations, and to Wendy Bass for her magnificent cover and display design.

A big thanks to George Rutkowski and Bob Reddig of PC Rents, for keeping me in computers.

My thanks and appreciation to my dear friend Marisa Berenson, for always nurturing my muse and providing me with space to work and live in when times were tough.

I am grateful to my parents and my sister for their love, concern, and help over the years.

Of course, a big thanks and love to my dear husband, Jim Walker, and my two little girls, Eleanor and Marisa, who are always so supportive, understanding, and patient when I'm writing. Without them there would be no balance in my life.

CONTENTS

With this book you have received one of the earth's most precious gifts: a clear quartz crystal. Beyond its beauty and clarity, your crystal is a tool of unlimited potential and power that you, the user, will determine. Since the energy potential of your crystal is so powerful, it is important that you use it only for your highest good and in positive ways.

Though *Crystal Clear* offers exercises, visualizations, and affirmations to enhance your well-being, this book is not designed to treat emotional disorders, depression, or other illnesses and should not be used in place of medical treatment or psychotherapy or counseling when they are indicated.

Several of the exercises in this book are intended to help vitalize the body, but for any health problems you should consult your physician for the best course of therapy.

INTRODUCTION

"It has been said
That each of us has
Deep within
The knowledge of all things.
And when we ready ourselves to remember this,
Then the knowledge is there to be known."

  —From the wisdom of the Essenes as revealed in
          the Dead Sea Scrolls

I was first introduced to the world of crystals about five years ago while living in New York City. I had been working on a book with a psychic astrologer, so I was primed: During the course of our collaboration, he had stimulated my curiosity and I was eager to explore the "other possibilities" in life. Then, shortly after the book was completed, a friend of mine called and urged me to see a psychic she knew who had recently moved from Hawaii to my Greenwich Village neighborhood. My friend sounded enchanted and transformed by her experience with the psychic, and before she hung up the phone she breathlessly exclaimed to me, "Wait until you see all the rocks she has!"

The psychic's name was Linda Waldron. When I called to schedule an appointment with her, I was nervous. I was suspicious of her deep, throaty cackle, and two days later, as I made my way along the winding West Village side streets, the wind off the Hudson River rattling the November leaves, I almost turned around and went home. But my curiosity got the better of me and I continued my journey.

When I arrived at Linda's apartment building I was not surprised to see that it was an old turn-of-the-century brownstone complete with gargoyles perched above the doorway. I took a deep breath before I let myself in and climbed six flights of stairs through dingy darkness.

I was totally unprepared for what I experienced as Linda opened her apartment door. I expected the worst, but instead I was greeted by a lively woman wearing every color in the rainbow—from the yellow scarf around her neck to the violet socks on her feet. As I entered her tiny apartment I was at once bedazzled by and bathed in beautiful, glowing, clean white light. I began to feel light and uplifted—as though I was receiving an energy transfusion.

Everywhere I looked there were rocks of all colors, shapes, and sizes filling every nook and cranny of her precious small space—amethysts, rose quartz, tourmalines, carnelians, and aquamarines. They were arranged in bowls, placed on shelves, piled on the counter, and neatly arranged in rows on her desk. Most amazing were the clear quartz crystals that filled her windows, catching and refracting beams of light—spilling colorful rainbows into the rooms. Magnificent crystal clusters as well as single crystals of all sizes lined the windowsills. Quartz crystal slivers and quartz crystal teardrops, each one gleaming like a rare precious jewel, hung in front of the window panes. I stood transfixed by these two small windows that overflowed with so much warmth and brightness.

As Linda chatted away, I barely heard a word she said. Instinctively I picked up one of the smaller quartz crystals from the windowsill and held it in my left hand. I felt a subtle vibration—a kind of humming in my palm. I looked at Linda in amazement, to which she responded, "I see you've found your crystal! Welcome to the light, welcome to the truth."

I looked at the crystal in my hand—the light, the truth? At first I didn't get it. Then with Linda's guidance and my own experimentation, I began to realize the crystal's potential to help me get in touch with myself— my light and my truth. My desires, my goals, and my wildest dreams began to come into focus, as well as the things that were holding me back from understanding who I really was and becoming the best person that I could be—my fears, anxieties, and my suppressed emotions. It was as if I were looking into a mirror and really seeing myself for the first time.

As I became "crystal friendly" I began to use my crystal to support and empower my positive thoughts and wishes. I held it, talked to it, imagined with it, kept it in my pocket whenever I could, meditated with it, and even slept with it under my pillow. I told it what I wanted, what I didn't want, and also confronted what it amplified about myself that I didn't particularly like. Buried emotions began to emerge and with the help of my crystal I began to release the negative feelings associated with them.

My crystal became my lucky charm, my rabbit's foot, my silent friend, my confidence booster, my companion in prayer, and my pocket shrink. It went with me to important meetings and when I worked as a ghostwriter, it helped me get through difficult celebrity interviews. Whenever I began to feel anxious or overwhelmed I would reach into my pocket and rub my crystal. The more I worked with it, the more uses I discovered it had. I found that with its energy and the clarity it brought it could help me make decisions, solve problems, and harmonize personal relationships. I found that my crystal was a master stress releaser, helping me relax a headache away.

Since that most unusual and wonderful day when I was first introduced to crystals, many crystals have come into my life. Some I have kept, but most I have passed on to friends and strangers in need. One of the great mysteries of the crystal is that it seems to go wherever it is most needed. You may have one for a month or maybe a year; but I have found that when your time with it is up it either disappears or you get an overwhelming urge to pass it on to someone else. I am convinced that part of the magic of crystals is that they instill a generosity of spirit in all of us.

It seems to me that crystals have numerous uses, and that each one has a unique story to tell and an energy to share. When you work with crystals you never stop learning—about yourself and about the power of crystal energy. What I offer in this book are guidelines to get you started. I am sharing with you what different teachers have taught me, what I have discovered on my own through experimentation, and general information that is common knowledge among crystal users. Keep in mind that there are no hard and fast rules to follow when working with your crystal. All that's required is that you be receptive to the crystal's energy and what it amplifies within your own being—*your* light and *your* truth.

Experiment and explore with an open heart and mind. Your crystal can become a tool for tranformation when it's coupled with the power of your mind, since its potential is ultimately determined by you, the user. Now take your crystal in hand and let the magic begin!

Connie Church

CRYSTAL CLEAR

CRYSTALS THROUGH THE AGES ◆ 1

THE CRYSTAL STORY

Look at your clear quartz crystal. It is the most common of all minerals and actually grows within the earth. A crystal is born when water and sand mix under specific temperature, pressure, and energy conditions. Its formation began about 200 million years ago in quartz veins and pockets that existed in sandstone deposits within the earth.

The secrets of this naturally faceted six-sided stone have mystified and enchanted different cultures and civilizations for thousands of years. Throughout history, the crystal has persevered as a symbol of power, salvation, and the universal life force of energy and light. Only recently have we begun to rediscover what had already been understood and used by so many ancient civilizations.

Ancient Egyptians, Druid priests, Tibetan monks, priests and kings of Christian Europe, and many American Indian tribes have considered the clear quartz crystal a sacred object of incredible power. For thousands of years crystals have been believed by many people to have healing properties, warding off enemies, protecting soldiers in battle, and even curing laziness. Christians once believed that clear quartz crystal was holy water from heaven that had frozen into ice on its way to earth. Miraculously, it was then petrified by the angels so that it would not melt, thus preserving the holy water to bless and protect mankind.

It is only in our day that quartz crystal has been used simply for self-adornment. Wearing crystal jewelry, which began in ancient Egypt, was initially for protection, healing, and self-empowerment. Mounted crystals would be worn at different parts of the body to heal and uplift the wearer. Necklaces were worn at the throat by people who found it difficult to speak; over the heart to increase self-love or compassion for others. Earrings, bracelets, and ankle bracelets were worn at acupuncture points to stimulate healing, and those who wore crystal jewelry could protect their souls from the intrusion of demons.

Druid priests thought that clear quartz crystal was a godlike force that could overcome all evil. In ancient Tibet it was believed that the eastern portion of heaven was composed of clear quartz crystal.

In medieval Europe people sought crystal for adornment as well as for its medicinal use. Kings wore crystals in their crowns so that they would govern more wisely and also because it created an aura of power and spirituality around them. And just as they wore crystals, they ingested them. In the Middle Ages, crystals were powdered and mixed with wine to treat numerous illnesses, including dysentery, diarrhea, colic, and gout.

Many American Indian medicine men used crystals for diagnosing illness and in their healing rituals—they considered the clear quartz crystal to be a "living rock" and "spirit helper." Quartz crystals that had rainbows within them were held by the dying Indian and used as a focal point for merging with the spirits. The dead were buried with precious crystal charms, believed to be valuable property.

In understanding the power, magic, and mystique that has been attributed to the crystal, no discussion of crystal history would be complete without mentioning the lost continent of Atlantis, which may or may not have existed. It is believed by many parapsychologists, archeologists, and scientists that the early civilization of this continent was highly advanced in spiritual and scientific knowledge through its use of crystal technology.

The Atlanteans are said to have developed a technology in which crystals were used to convert the sun's energy into a form of free electricity that even made possible interdimensional communication and travel. Legend has it that there were beautiful healing temples erected in Atlantis where colors and vibrations were channeled and integrated through crystals to create light-based healing techniques. With the help of crystals diseases were diagnosed, tissues and limbs regenerated, and all forms of disease cured. It is also believed that crystals were used to prevent the physical body from aging. Ultimately the entire civilization revolved around the crystal's real ability to transmit, transform, amplify, and focus energy.

Eventually the great crystal power that was the life force of Atlantis was perverted by those in positions of authority. There are stories of mind control and hypnosis of the masses using beams of crystal energy. As crystals evolved into weapons of war, they were used to destroy and enslave. In the process mighty energies were released, leading to a complete imbalance within the earth's electromagnetic field. It is believed that this misuse of power culminated in a massive earthquake, leading to the final destruction and sinking of Atlantis.

COMMONLY HELD BELIEFS ABOUT THE POWER OF CRYSTALS

Behind all the legends, myths, and mysticism, crystals are said to have special characteristics that are now being actively explored. Clear quartz crystal is in fact a powerhouse capable of absorbing, transforming, transmitting, amplifying, and focusing energy. This capacity is not the result of any magical power the crystal may or may not have. The laws of energy and nature determine this function, which becomes especially powerful when combined with the magic of our mental energy.

Perfect in its molecular structure, clear quartz crystal aligns with the magnetic fields of the earth. When squeezed and released, even in the palm of your hand, it produces small amounts of electricity that vibrate with both a positive and a negative energy field. In fact, the photo on the cover of this book is a *Kirlian* photograph, which actually shows the crystal's vibrating energy. The precision of this vibrating or oscillating energy field has made radio, satellite communications, telephone, and television possible. Currently, crystals are used in computer technology to expand storage capacity—eventually it will be possible for all of the books in the Library of Congress to be stored in a space equivalent to the size of a refrigerator.

A crystal in its natural state can enhance your aesthetic and physical environment. Many people feel that just having crystals around makes them feel good—and justifiably so. As each crystal naturally vibrates its own energy, it energizes its environment and anyone within close proximity. Crystals also emit negative ions which help create uplifting and harmonious feelings. As a personal tool for transformation, crystals can be used to amplify, store, transmit, and focus your thoughts, emotions, and desires—ultimately manifesting them into reality.

Given their interesting history, valuable technological use, and real power, it's easy to understand why people are going crystal crazy! Many crystal experts think of the eighties as the new stone age, as we tap into the vast resources of the crystal kingdom to rediscover their power.

Before you bought this book, you probably looked through all the *Crystal Clear* books available. Finally, you picked the book that contained the crystal that appealed to you most. Perhaps you chose it because it was thin, or fat, or exceptionally clear, or maybe it was rather cloudy. Maybe you detected within it the hint of a rainbow, sparkling through the plastic as you held it up to the light. Just as you chose the crystal, it chose you by matching its energy with yours. Believe it or not, in its own special way the crystal you have selected vibrates with an energy that is mutually attracted to yours. Think of it as an energy connection between you and your crystal.

If you received this book and crystal as a gift, then the crystal matched its energy with you through the person who bought it for you. Although indirect, the energy connection was made between you and your crystal.

Your crystal comes from one of the major crystal mines in Brazil. While every crystal has a unique energy of its own, there are general qualities that crystals share, depending on the mines or deposits they come from. Brazilian crystals, like yours, are older crystals known for their focused, predictable energy.

Crystals are also mined in great abundance from deposits in Arkansas and Madagascar. Arkansas crystals are younger and have a quick, scattered energy. Many experts feel that they are not as focused in their energy as are the Brazilian and Madagascarian crystals. Like the Brazilian crystals, those mined in Madagascar are older with a focused, powerful, steady energy.

CLEANING, CLEARING, AND CHARGING YOUR CRYSTAL

Before you begin working with your crystal you should clean it to clear it of any energy patterns or vibrations it picked up and stored before it came to you. There are many methods you can use, all of which are considered

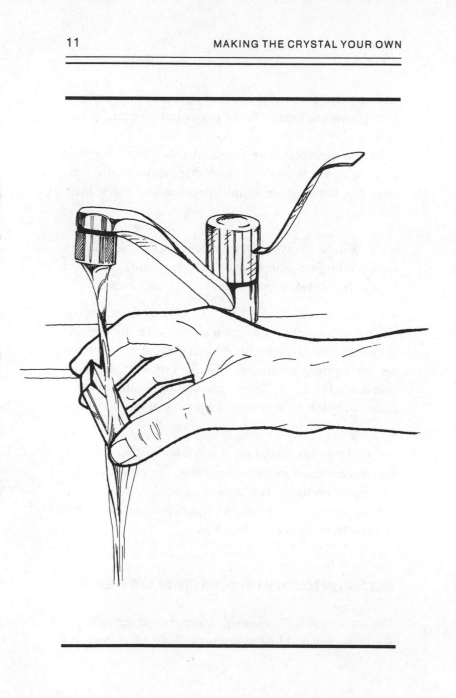

an important part of the ritual of crystal care. These will be explained in further detail in the last chapter, "Crystal Care."

In the meantime I recommend this quick cleaning, clearing, and charging method that requires only running tap water, some simple visualization and a little sunlight:

• • • With your crystal in your right hand, hold it under cool running tap water for about one minute. Hold on to it tightly between your thumb and index finger.

• • • As the water runs over your crystal, imagine that the water is running through it as well, literally washing it crystal clear. Imagine that everything it encountered on its journey to you is rushing out of the crystal and down the drain. While one minute is all it takes to clean and clear it, continue longer if you feel it's necessary.

• • • Place your crystal on a windowsill or anywhere it can receive direct sunlight for at least ten minutes. Crystals thrive on light. You may even want to stick it outside on a porch or terrace. For a supercharge, place it in the sun from noon until two P.M.

GETTING IN TOUCH WITH YOUR CRYSTAL'S ENERGY

Once your crystal is cleaned, cleared, and charged, examine it closely. Hold it up to the light. Are there any

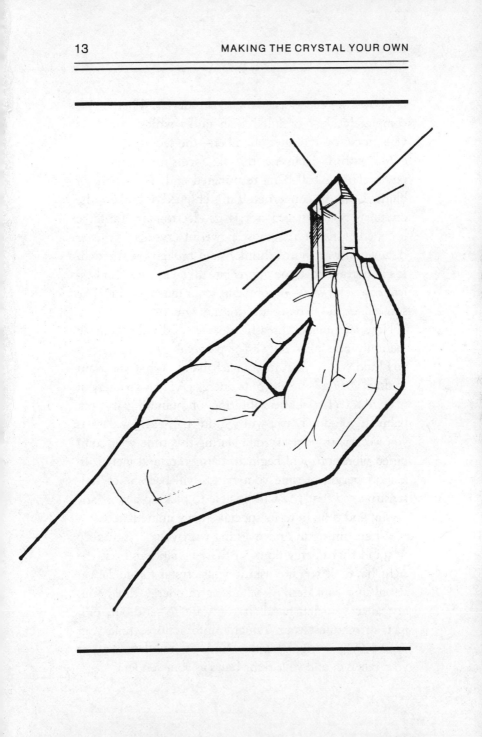

rainbows or reflections dancing inside it? Whether it's completely clear or filled with milky white wisps and veils, focus on its inner chamber—the secret world that exists within. Examine the six facets that create its point. This is called its terminated end. Is it sharp or blunt? Don't be concerned if it is chipped or broken; the crystal is not damaged nor is its electromagnetic force lessened. One of the most powerful crystals I've ever discovered was short, chunky, and broken on the end. It's important that you appreciate all your crystal's physical characteristics—appreciate its uniqueness. Just like snowflakes, no two crystals are the same.

Now sit quietly, breathe deeply, and calm yourself mentally and physically in a peaceful environment as you hold your crystal in your left hand. What you want to do is attune yourself to its energy. At first you may or may not feel a subtle vibration or humming in your palm. If you don't, you will within the next few days as you work with your crystal. During this time your combined vibrations will begin to harmonize and merge. In a short period of time your hands will become crystal-sensitive, so that you will be able to pick up almost any crystal and tune in to its special energy immediately.

When tuning in and working with your crystal keep in mind that energy flows in the left hand and out the right hand. If you are asking your crystal for guidance, visualizing your desires, or taking in energy, hold your crystal in your left hand. If you want to send out, project, or manifest your thoughts into actions, hold your crystal in your right hand. Think of your left hand as your receiver and your right hand as your sender.

DEVELOPING YOUR INNER VOICE

One of the most amazing, magical, and important aspects of crystal work is that it helps develop your inner voice as it amplifies your mental energy. The inner voice means different things to different people. Some of you may think of it as your intuition, your gut feeling, or your sixth sense. It may make itself apparent to you through an intuitive feeling, a vision or vivid mental picture, or a subtle verbal response that only you can hear.

Regardless of how you define it or perceive it, it is very important that you don't deny it. Your inner voice can provide solutions to your problems and resolutions to any conflicts you might have. Many crystal users interpret this as the crystal talking to them and guiding them—so listen carefully and seriously consider what you hear. Trust your inner voice.

PERSONALIZING YOUR CRYSTAL

In order to use your crystal most effectively you need to personalize it so that your vibrations are attuned to it and its vibrations are attuned to you. The best way to do this is to keep it on you or with you at all times during the first thirty days you have it. Pocket or purse, it doesn't matter—just make sure it's always with you. This includes sleeping with it as well as bathing or showering with it.

When you go to bed you can place the crystal under

your pillow or you can fall asleep with it in your left hand. If you fall asleep with it in your hand, don't be surprised if you're still holding it when you wake up. Or you may wake up to find your crystal under the sheet at the bottom of your bed.

Whether you shower or take a bath, don't hesitate to include your crystal. Simply slip it in the water with you —an added benefit is that it energizes the water and vitalizes you, giving you an energy lift. Or if you are showering, place it on the tub's edge and allow the water to run over it.

At the end of the thirty-day period your energy will have merged with the energy of your crystal. It is not necessary to keep your crystal with you at all times to utilize its power fully, but you may want to keep it with you anyway. It is good to have "at hand" to ward off anxiety attacks. I like to have one with me just to help keep me calm and balance my energy.

Your crystal will communicate to you what is best. Listen to your inner voice. Some crystals I have worked with seemed to have a permanent place in my pocket, while others stayed on my bedside table when not in use.

SHOULD ANYONE ELSE TOUCH OR USE YOUR CRYSTAL?

Many crystal users feel that allowing someone else to handle or use their crystal makes them vulnerable—as though they are giving away their personal power. While it is true that when another person touches your crystal his or her energy is imprinted on it, I don't believe that anyone can take away your personal power unless you want them to have it.

Personally, I only allow people I love or whose energy I admire to hold and look at my crystal. One of my friends is a loving, happy person who is a professional comedian. I love his energy and he always makes me laugh, so I never hesitate to let him hold my crystal. But no one actually uses my crystal. And people I have contact with who are negative, bitter, or depressed never even see my crystal. It stays in my pocket where its vibrations effectively protect me from and deflect any negativity that may be coming my way.

If, inadvertently, your crystal is handled and you don't feel comfortable with the energy imparted, cleanse it, clear it, and recharge it. Once you've done this, you can begin working with it again.

Your crystal is your tool for transformation as well as your personal support system. It can help you to balance your energies, control stress, release unpleasant emotions, improve your concentration and mental clarity, build confidence, and harmonize your personal relationships. As you tune in to the vast resources of your inner self and take control of your energy, your body, mind, and spirit will be vitalized. But before you begin working with your crystal you need to understand some basics. Specifically they are: deep breathing, visualizing, affirming, and programming your crystal.

THE IMPORTANCE OF PROPER DEEP BREATHING

Breath is our life force, activating all body movement and aiding in all of our body functions. Unfortunately most of us live on minimal, shallow breaths. It is as though we are afraid to take life in fully, depriving ourselves of the benefits of good deep breathing. Not only does deep breathing help our heart and lungs work more effectively, it also brings about a deep sense of relaxation, focus, harmony, and center.

When working with your crystal it is important that you tune in to the moment and calm your mind so that you can get in touch with your inner voice and center your energy. Focusing on your breathing, through gentle, deep breathing, is the most effective way to do this.

The following deep breathing technique can be practiced often and, while the body position will vary, should be followed whenever you are instructed to "breathe deeply" or "begin your deep breathing" in the chapters that follow.

• • • Lie down on a comfortable flat surface with your legs stretched out and your hands resting comfortably at your side. (Be careful if you have back problems.)

• • • First begin with a slow, deep inhalation through your nose to the count of 1-2-3-4-5-6-7-8. Bring your breath from your chest, into your stomach and then into your abdomen.

• • • Now slowly exhale through your mouth to the count of 1-2-3-4-5-6-7-8, feeling your abdomen contract. Visualize your breath with your eyes, hear it with your ears, and feel it throughout your body.

• • • Repeat the entire process.

• • • As you continue your deep breathing, become the breath—nothing more. Flow with it. Feel the quieting of your body, mind, and spirit.

UNDERSTANDING VISUALIZATION

Visualization is a process in which you create in your mind a clear mental picture of what you would like to have happen in your life. You might want to think of it as focused or directed imagination that has an intention. When you visualize you are structuring your thoughts so that they can become a reality.

The power of visualization is based on the principle that form follows idea—that thoughts are things. When you take an idea or thought and repeatedly visualize it in your mind, it can attract and become that reality on the material plane.

You may find that you "see" very clearly when you

visualize, or that you are only able to think about what you are trying to imagine. However, as you use your crystal to empower your visualizations, your ability to visualize with vivid mental pictures will improve.

You will be using two different types of visualization: active and passive. In using active visualization you will consciously create mental pictures and then send the energy of those pictures out into the universe, with the help of your crystal, so that they can become a reality. You will use passive visualization, interpreting the images that float freely into your mind, when you are problem solving, releasing negative emotions, or dealing with depression.

STRUCTURING YOUR AFFIRMATIONS

In taking your visualizations from thought to concrete reality, it is important to support them with affirmations. When you affirm a thought or idea you are literally "making firm" and strengthening your intention. Think of affirming as simply stating *what is;* and when used during crystal work, your crystal will support the affirmation through amplification.

Affirmations can be verbal, written down, or quietly thought. I think saying or writing affirmations gives them more power, although there are times when it may be impossible to do either one. In these situations, just repeat your affirmation over and over again in your mind.

In structuring your affirmations keep them simple, direct, positive, and always construct them in the <u>present tense</u>—as though what you are saying is already so. For instance, if you are looking for a new job, and visualizing what that job is, your affirmation would be:

"I have a new job that is perfect for me"
not
"I will find a new job that is perfect for me."

It is also important that you put as much energy and real belief into your affirmation as is possible. If negative feelings and doubt are creating a block, then write your affirmation out over and over again until you feel that you are starting to believe what you are affirming.

PROGRAMMING YOUR CRYSTAL

It's easy to program your crystal continuously to hold and affirm your visualizations. Simply hold your crystal up to your third eye—your sixth *chakra,* which is located above your nose and between your brows—as you visualize your desire. (I'll explain more about *chakras* in the next chapter.) Now imagine that you are projecting that desire into your crystal.

For example: If you have an important interview for a new job and you're feeling very nervous, hold your crystal to your third eye and visualize yourself as calm, confident, and secure in your abilities. Play out the whole

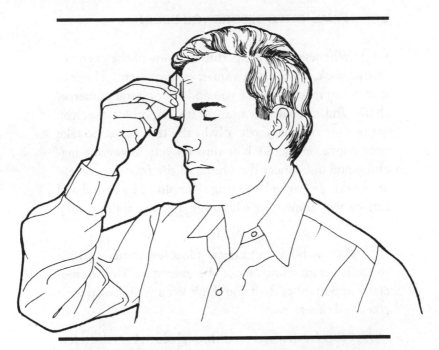

scenario in your mind, seeing yourself at the interview
—at ease with the situation.

Now project this visualization into your crystal. Finish
by sitting quietly, as you mentally affirm your visualization. It might be something like this: "I am confident,
poised, and serene as I am interviewed."

When you actually go to the interview, you can hold
your crystal and receive your visualization and the affirmation it emanates back to you. Think of your crystal as
your special assistant and personal support system.

■   ■   ■

SOME FINAL NOTES BEFORE YOU BEGIN

• • • Whenever you are performing any of the exercises in this book, try to be in a quiet environment. Think of it as your private time for you and your crystal to merge, share, and mutually "vibrate." It's important that you are not interrupted, especially by the telephone. So take your phone off the hook or turn on your answering machine and disconnect the phone in the room where you are working. A telephone ring is amplified by crystal and can be very unnerving when you are in a state of deep relaxation.

• • • Always hold your crystal for a few minutes to activate it before doing any of the exercises. This is especially important to do if you don't keep your crystal with you at all times.

• • • I suggest that you read through each exercise a few times and become familiar with it before you actually do it.

Like you, each crystal has its own unique vibration, operating at a specific frequency. As it vibrates from its state of perfection (remember that it is perfect in its molecular structure), it can perfect all that is around it. When the vibrations of the crystal interact and merge with yours, a natural healing occurs. It is the crystal's basic function to create harmony, peace, and a general sense of well-being wherever it goes simply by balancing each energy with which it comes in contact. And there is no doubt that a balanced energy system is essential to your well-being.

UNDERSTANDING YOUR ENERGY SYSTEM

It is believed that each of us has seven major energy centers in our bodies, called *chakras*, where there is an increased vital force. Combined, they make up your energy system. This energy system is responsible for moving and distributing the universal life energy throughout your body. When your body is free of tension and stress, this energy flows naturally and keeps the body balanced.

The knowledge of the chakras dates back thousands of years. When the healers and seers of early civilizations observed these energies they interpreted them as spinning wheels of light—hence the term chakra, which in Sanskrit means "wheel."

Each chakra corresponds to a specific area of the body, a gland, a color, and different aspects of human behavior that define the levels of our consciousness. Depending on your level of consciousness at the moment, this is the chakra you are currently operating from—or how you are directing your energy.

It is your level of consciousness that determines the different kinds of thoughts, people, and situations that you attract into your life. If any of these bring with them negative or unpleasant moments, the corresponding chakra can become blocked. Also, through the years, memories, emotional pain, and unresolved and re-

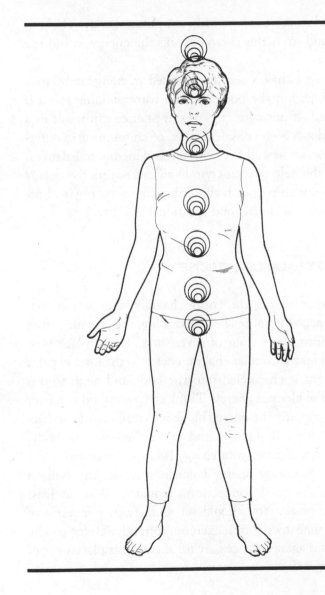

pressed emotions stay within the physical body. The tension and stress this creates blocks the energy within the chakras.

When a chakra becomes blocked an energy imbalance occurs within the body and the corresponding gland is affected. If not corrected this imbalance can result in a breakdown of the physical body, often resulting in different diseases as well as emotional and mental imbalances. With the help of your crystal you can restore the energy balance within your body, enhancing your physical fitness, mental clarity, and emotional stability.

ENERGY BALANCE EXERCISE

Like your crystal, the entire chakra system within your body acts like a prism—separating the cosmic white light into a spectrum of seven rays. If you place your crystal on a particular chakra, energy in the form of color and light is channeled into the body and helps to dissolve the blocked energy. Think of your crystal as a laser beam, zapping the energy block into millions of particles that can easily disperse and move through your body. Once this is done, your energy balance is restored.

The following energy balance exercise, involving a chakra-to-crystal connection, should be done at least once a week. You should set aside twenty minutes of quiet time to do this exercise correctly. Refer to the chakra diagram if necessary for the correct placement of your crystal.

Color & Chakra	Location	Positive Qualities	Negative Qualities
1st Red	sex organs, rectum	activity, spontaneity, leadership, independence, manifesting on earth plane, alert, pioneer spirit	anger, violence, revenge, impulsive, constantly active, manipulative, sexually obsessive
2nd Orange	pelvis/spleen	confidence, courage, socially assertive, inventive, hospitable, warm, ambitious	inferiority/superiority, sluggish, pompous, cruel, values social status, ostentatious, social climbing
3rd Yellow	stomach/solar plexus	active intelligence, organization, clarity of mind, discipline, logical, analytical, efficient	lazy, cowardly, judgmental, cynical, always planning, never manifesting, nit-picky
4th Green	heart center	generous, accepting, sharing, compassionate, expansive, nurturing, secure, growth	jealous, miserly, possessive, emotionally and financially insecure, envious, resistant to change, unable to love oneself
5th Blue	throat	patient, peaceful, serene, devotional, loyal, ability to verbalize, speak truth, idealistic	ultra-conservative, clings to tradition, depressed, isolation, melancholic, slow to respond, unable to verbalize clearly
6th Purple	third eye (above nose, between brows)	intuitive, perceptive, telepathic, optimistic, meditative, visionary	superstitious, spaced-out, easily fascinated, fears the dark unconscious, unable to be in the moment
7th White	crown (top of head)	creative, mystical, charming, magic, world service, ritual, humanitarian	daydreamy, uses power to overwhelm others, needs to be idolized, arrogant, conceited

—Used by permission of Zoe Artemis

• • • Lie down on a comfortable flat surface. Bend your knees so that your lower back feels relaxed. When you are not placing your crystal on one of your chakras, rest your arms in a relaxed position at your side, palms up.

• • • Place your crystal on your first chakra—your pubic area (the center of how you feel about being alive). Begin your deep breathing.

• • • As you deeply inhale, know that you are consciously breathing in the vital life force, positive thoughts, love, and good health. As you deeply exhale, breathe out all negative thoughts, worries, and anxieties —just let it all go. Continue this process as you feel the quieting of your body, mind, and spirit—and make sure that you breathe deeply throughout the entire exercise.

• • • Now focus your attention on your first chakra. Imagine that your crystal is drawing into your body a beautiful beam of red light. Feel its energy and warmth penetrate your first chakra, as it dissolves any blocked energy that might exist.

• • • Continue to focus your attention on your first chakra, and as you deeply exhale say the following affirmation out loud or silently: "I love my body, my life and the world around me." *Or:* "I have the energy and vitality to accomplish my goals."

• • • Repeat the affirmation each time you deeply exhale. Do this seven times. Now finish by saying, "So it is."

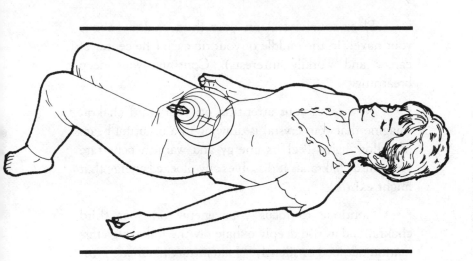

• • • Place your crystal on your second chakra—on your abdomen, below your navel (the center of courage and self-confidence). Continue your deep breathing.

• • • Now focus your attention on your second chakra. Imagine that your crystal is drawing into your body a beautiful beam of orange light. Feel its energy and warmth penetrate your second chakra, as it dissolves any blocked energy that might exist.

• • • Continue to focus your attention on your second chakra, and as you deeply exhale say the following affirmation out loud or silently: "I am now creating my life exactly as I want it." Or: "I have the courage and confidence to move ahead and meet life's challenges."

• • • Repeat the affirmation each time you deeply exhale. Do this seven times. Now finish by saying, "So it is."

• • • Place your crystal on your third chakra—above your navel, in the middle of your rib cage (the center of career and worldly interests). Continue your deep breathing.

• • • Now focus your attention on your third chakra. Imagine that your crystal is drawing in a beautiful beam of yellow light. Feel its energy and warmth penetrate your third chakra, as it dissolves any blocked energy that might exist.

• • • Continue to focus your energy on your third chakra, and as you deeply exhale say the following affirmation out loud or silently: "I am attracting divine prosperity and success." *Or:* "I accept all the joy and abundance that life is offering me."

• • • Repeat the affirmation each time you deeply exhale. Do this seven times. Now finish by saying, "So it is."

• • • Place your crystal on your fourth chakra—the middle of your chest at your breastbone (the center of relationships). Continue your deep breathing.

• • • Now focus your attention on your fourth chakra. Imagine that your crystal is drawing into your body a beautiful beam of green light. Feel its energy and warmth penetrate your fourth chakra, as it dissolves any blocked energy that might exist.

• • • Continue to focus your attention on your fourth chakra, and as you deeply exhale say the following affirmation out loud or silently: "I let go of the past, and I love myself just the way I am." *Or (filling in the appropriate name and action):* "I forgive _____ for being _____. I forgive you and release you."

• • • Repeat the affirmation each time you deeply exhale. Do this seven times. Now finish by saying, "So it is."

• • • Place your crystal on your fifth chakra—at the base of your throat (the center of communication). Continue your deep breathing.

• • • Now focus your attention on your fifth chakra. Imagine that your crystal is drawing into your body a beautiful beam of blue light. Feel its energy and warmth penetrate your fifth chakra, as it dissolves any blocked energy that might exist.

• • • Continue to focus your attention on your fifth chakra, and as you deeply exhale say the following affirmation out loud or silently: "I communicate clearly, honestly, and with love." *Or:* "I am relaxed and centered."

• • • Repeat the affirmation each time you deeply exhale. Do this seven times. Now finish by saying, "So it is."

• • • Place your crystal on your sixth chakra or third eye —between the eyebrows, above the nose (the center of intuition and clairvoyance). Continue your deep breathing.

• • • Now focus your attention on your sixth chakra. Imagine that your crystal is drawing into your body a beautiful beam of purple light. Feel its energy and warmth penetrate your sixth chakra, as it dissolves any blocked energy that might exist.

• • • Continue to focus your attention on your sixth chakra, and as you deeply exhale say the following affirmation out loud or silently: "My higher power guides me in everything I do." *Or:* "I am attuned to the divine order of my life."

• • • Repeat the affirmation each time you deeply exhale. Do this seven times. Now finish by saying, "So it is."

• • • Place your crystal on your seventh chakra—the top of your head (the center of enlightenment and service). Since the seventh chakra is at the crown of your head, simply place the crystal against the top of your head. Continue your deep breathing.

• • • Now focus your attention on your seventh chakra. Imagine that your crystal is drawing into your body, from the top of your head, a beautiful beam of white light. Feel its energy and warmth penetrate your seventh chakra, as it dissolves any blocked energy that might exist.

• • • Continue to focus your attention on your seventh chakra, and as you deeply exhale say the following affirmation out loud or silently: "Divine light and love flow through me to everyone and everything around me." *Or:* "God and me, me and God are one." *Or:* I am the great opulence of God."

• • • Repeat the affirmation each time you deeply exhale. Do this seven times. Now finish by saying, "So it is."

• • • Remove your crystal from the top of your head and hold it in your left hand at your side as you relax. Rest quietly for a few minutes before getting up.

YOUR "MORNING GROUND"

Before you begin your day one of the best things you can do for yourself is what I call a "morning ground." Basically what this exercise does for you is focus and center your energy—the best possible way to start your day! There is nothing worse than leaving the house feeling like you're running off in a million directions. The more focused your energy is in the morning, the more you are likely to accomplish.

One of the nicest parts of this exercise is that you can do it before you get out of bed. This provides you with a smoother transition from your rested state to your active state, and it will leave you feeling less frazzled. There is nothing better than starting your day peacefully.

Once the alarm clock goes off, reach for your crystal. If you sleep with it under your pillow, it should be easy to find. Otherwise, you may find yourself searching the sheets—don't worry; it's there somewhere.

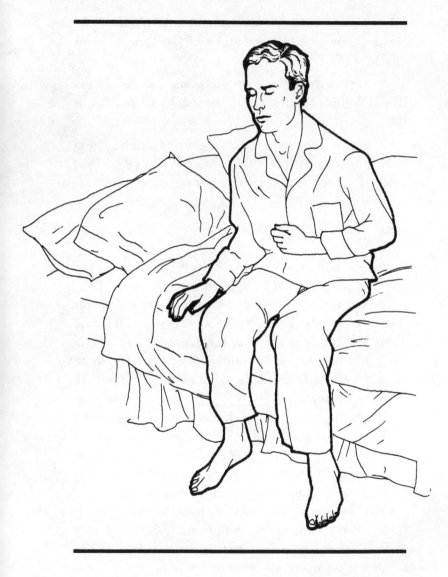

• • • Sit up straight on the edge of your bed with your feet flat on the floor. Hold your crystal in your left hand, resting it next to your solar plexus, above your navel. This way you are connecting with your third chakra.

• • • Begin your deep breathing. (Eight counts in and eight counts out.)

• • • As you inhale visualize that your whole body is filling with a glorious golden light that you are drawing in through your nose.

• • • As you exhale say the following affirmation out loud or silently: "I am centered and at one with my energy."

• • • Continue your visualization as you inhale and your affirmation as you exhale seven times.

• • • Now visualize the golden light flowing through you, as it travels down your torso, down your legs and to your feet.

• • • See and feel that your whole body is glowing with this golden light. Imagine the warmth and sense your well-being.

• • • Now visualize the golden light flowing through the soles of your feet, into the floor, and then through the floor until it penetrates deep into the earth. See, feel, and know that you are grounded to the earth.

• • • Hold this visualization as you again affirm, as you exhale, seven times: "I am centered and at one with my energy."

LISTING

After your morning ground, it is the perfect time to organize your energy and the activities of your day with a mental exercise I have called "listing." This effectively replaces the standard "daily list" or "things to do" that most of us write down every day. "Listing" before you begin the activities of your day helps you flow effortlessly from one task to the next, without having to ask "What do I need to do next?" Also, if you're constantly running in ten different directions trying to get everything done yet completing nothing, this is the perfect exercise for you.

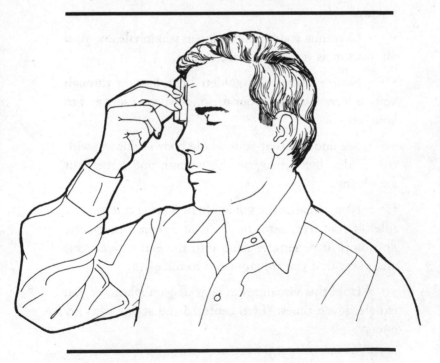

• • • You can do your listing either sitting up in bed or sitting back in a comfortable chair. With your left hand hold your crystal on your sixth chakra (above the nose and between the brows).

• • • Breathe deeply as you relax into the pulse of your crystal.

• • • First mentally list and visualize everything that you would *like to* accomplish for that day. As you visualize, see yourself performing each activity. Your list might be something like this:

—change the catlitter

—water the plants

—exercise

—pick up a gift for Diane during my lunch break

—catch up on my backlog of paperwork

—begin the financial report that is due next week

—call mom

—do a load of wash

—pay my bills

—talk with my boss about next week's meeting

• • • From your mental list, pick out the activities you feel *must be done* and prioritize them. Your list might now be something like this:

—change the cat litter

—exercise

—talk with my boss about next week's meeting

—begin the financial report that is due next week

—call mom

—pay my bills

• • • Now visualize yourself performing each activity, in order, on the *must-be-done* list.

• • • Remove your crystal from your sixth chakra and hold it in your right hand. (Remember that your right hand, as the sender, projects your thoughts into actions.)

• • • Visualize your *must-be-done* list one more time and then affirm: "So be it."

The list has now been clarified in your mind and programmed into your crystal. Through its amplification, the crystal will empower your mental list and guide you through your day. If you begin to hesitate at any point during the day, hold your crystal in your left hand for a few minutes and you will continue to complete one activity after another.

Although your crystal stimulates, enhances, and empowers your mental abilities, at first you might find this exercise difficult because it will take some real mental effort on your part to remember the list as you prioritize it. But the more often you perform "listing," the easier it will get. Your list will probably also increase. An added benefit of this exercise is that it enhances your mental clarity and your organizational ability.

STRESS RELEASE

Besides balancing your energy system at least once a week it is important to release any accumulated stress at the end of each day. Think of this exercise as daily maintenance for your well-being. After performing it every day for two weeks, you will be amazed by how much better you feel. Any symptoms of stress and tension you had will lessen and may even vanish completely. You'll find yourself getting fewer headaches and having a calmer, steadier energy.

The ideal maintenance program, to keep your energy balanced and flowing, is to begin your day with the "morning ground" and end it with this "stress release" exercise. This exercise can also be performed at any point in your day if you're having an anxiety attack or just feeling overwhelmed by all you need to accomplish.

• • • Lie down on a comfortable flat surface. Bend your knees so that your lower back feels relaxed. Place your crystal on your sixth chakra (between the brows, above the nose). The terminated end should be pointed up

toward the crown of your head. Rest your arms in a relaxed position at your side, palms up.

• • • Begin your deep breathing. Become the breath—nothing more. Flow with it. Now focus on your crystal, feeling its subtle vibrations calm your mind. Spend a few minutes relaxing into the rhythm of your deep breathing and your crystal's vibrations.

• • • As you flow into a state of deep relaxation, tune into any tense areas of your body. Repeatedly affirm to yourself: "I am stress-free."

• • • Continue the affirmation while visualizing that your crystal is drawing in soothing beams of blue light from the core of the earth and through the soles of your feet.

• • • See the light flow up your legs, through your body, down your arms, and into your head—imagine your whole body filled and vibrating with this light.

• • • Now imagine your crystal drawing all of this vibrating light into it, bringing with it all of the accumulated stress and tension that is in your body.

• • • Knowing that all of your stress and tension is now contained within your crystal, not your body, continue your deep breathing and affirm: "I am stress-free."

• • • Remove the crystal from your forehead. Continue lying quietly, breathing deeply. Focus on your sense of lightness and well-being. Before you get up once again affirm, "I am stress-free."

• • • After this exercise it is important to clear your crystal of all the negative energy it has just accumulated. Place it under cold running tap water for at least thirty seconds, as you visualize your stress and tension washing out of your crystal and down the drain.

Even if you do nothing with your crystal but carry it with you, over a period of time you will begin to notice subtle changes in yourself. Your concentration will improve as your thoughts become more focused and clear. Not only will you feel physically and mentally vitalized, but your dreams may become more vivid and your imagination more active. Buried feelings and past emotional hurts may begin to surface—which will provide the opportunity for you to confront what's been lurking in your subconscious mind. They surface because your crystal amplifies even the most subtle mental energy. It is as though your crystal is all-seeing and all-knowing.

Any emotional conflicts you experience that you are unable to release affect your chakras, blocking your flow of energy. Until the conflicts are resolved and released, chances are good that the chakra will remain blocked. As I discussed in the previous chapter, blocked chakras can cause an energy imbalance and lead to disease.

It is your crystal's tendency to make right what's wrong, as it naturally balances whatever comes into its energy field. So listen closely to the thoughts, feelings, and impressions your crystal amplifies. These are your clues to your inner self, and they can help you understand what's motivating your desires, feelings, and actions. Once you understand the emotions that are directing your actions, it's easier to make necessary changes that will help quiet the conflicts. Most of us have within ourselves the ability to be our own therapists—often, all we have to do is listen and take the time to make sense of what we hear, so that we can then release it and be free of it.

CONFRONTING AND RELEASING NEGATIVE EMOTIONS

In this exercise, as you place your crystal on your fourth chakra (the heart chakra) you can expect suppressed and unresolved traumas, emotions, and even insecurities from your childhood to surface if they exist. While the emotions you feel may totally overwhelm you, and even bring you to tears, allow yourself to experience them fully. Once this is done, a catharsis begins to occur. You can then release the upset and negativity surrounding these emotions that have been buried deep within you.

It is very important that you allow yourself plenty of time to perform this exercise and that you perform it when you are alone. If nothing surfaces the first few times you do this, don't assume you are trauma-free— eventually something will become apparent. Sometimes fear of the past can hold back the emotions and delay their release.

Not only is this an effective exercise to release painful past memories, but it can also help you deal with any current emotional upheaval or problems.

• • • Lie down on a comfortable flat surface. Bend your knees so that your lower back feels relaxed. Place your crystal, terminated end toward your head, on your heart chakra. Rest your arms in a relaxed position at your side.

• • • Begin your deep breathing. Become the breath— nothing more. Flow with it. Feel the quieting of your body, mind, and spirit. Spend a few moments relaxing deeply into your breath. Perhaps you can feel the pulsing of your crystal on your heart chakra.

• • • As you continue with your deep breathing simply ask yourself the following questions, allowing yourself plenty of time between each question, and see how your inner self responds. Fully express whatever you feel, re- membering that this is your time to "let it all go."

—What's going on for me emotionally?

—Is anyone causing me emotional pain? If so, how? What role do I play?

—What is not working for me in my life?

—What part of my life needs clarity?

—What is making me angry?

And the final question:

—What am I physically feeling?

• • • If you feel tensions surfacing—maybe you are experiencing a tightness in your throat, a heaviness in your chest, a dull throb in your head—use your deep breathing to release these tense areas. As you take yourself through this process, make sure you continuously breathe deeply. When you hold on to your breath you are holding on to painful memories. Your deep breathing can facilitate the necessary release.

• • • Once you've expressed all you're feeling, inhale deeply and visualize that you are taking in the vital life force, love, good health, and positive thoughts. As you exhale release any negative thoughts, worries, and emotional pain that have surfaced. Let your breath all the way out. Continue this until you feel calm, centered, and at ease.

• • • Now continue your deep breathing, and as you exhale affirm out loud or silently: "I release all hurts both real and imagined. The life and the love of the universe flow through me and wash me clean." Repeat this seven times on seven deep exhalations.

• • • Imagine that your crystal is drawing into your heart a beautiful beam of loving pink light. See and feel this pink light fill your body. Know that the pink light is bathing your body with total love and understanding. Feel the love and let your body flow with it.

• • • Finish with this final affirmation, repeating it as many times as you wish: "I love myself just the way I am."

• • • Rest for five minutes before you get up.

If you have been in a state of depression, this exercise may boost your spirits. When you become depressed it is usually because you're turning the anger you feel back on yourself. I think of depression as anger turned "inside out." This can stifle your motivation, drive, and general zest for life. It is as though you are in a time warp, feeling unable to get out.

But when you get in touch with your anger, understand it, and explore all you're feeling and then release it, your depression has a way of suddenly disappearing. Accepting yourself is an important part of ridding yourself of depression. As you continuously affirm, "I love myself just the way I am," you begin to feel worthy of living actively again and reaping the benefits of life's riches.

CHANGING NEGATIVE BEHAVIOR TRAITS

Each of us probably has one or more negative behavior traits that get the better of us from time to time, and may even be holding us back personally or professionally. These traits correspond to the different chakras and occur when the energy associated with a particular chakra has taken on negative qualities. (Refer to the chakra chart on page 29.)

Some examples:

Impatience—first chakra (red), positive opposite: Patience

Low self-esteem—second chakra (orange), positive opposite: Self-confidence

Laziness—third chakra (yellow), positive opposite: Activity

Jealousy—fourth chakra (green), positive opposite: Acceptance

Disloyalty—fifth chakra (blue), positive opposite: Loyalty

Superstition—sixth chakra (purple), positive opposite: Intuition

Arrogance—seventh chakra (white), positive opposite: Humility

You might want to take a personal inventory and list any negative traits you feel you have. Referring to the chakra chart, match each trait to the corresponding chakra and its color by comparing it with the negative qualities listed.

Once you have your list of negative traits, or personality problems, and their corresponding chakras, you are ready to get to work—think of this as a self-improvement exercise! It's a good idea to address one trait at a time, and work on it for a week before moving on to the next one. Old habits and behavior patterns are not changed overnight.

Regardless of the negative trait, you follow the same format in this exercise—just plug in the particular trait, its chakra and color, and the visualization of the problems you encounter because of this trait. I will demonstrate this exercise with *impatience.*

• • • Lie down on a comfortable flat surface. Bend your knees so that your lower back feels relaxed. Begin your deep breathing.

• • • With your negative trait in mind, place your crystal on the corresponding chakra. (With impatience in mind, I place my crystal on my first chakra.)

• • • Imagine a colored beam of light, determined by the chakra, coming from your crystal and vibrating the chakra. (I imagine a red beam of light coming from my crystal and vibrating my first chakra.)

• • • Now think of your negative trait and visualize the different problems you have recently encountered be-

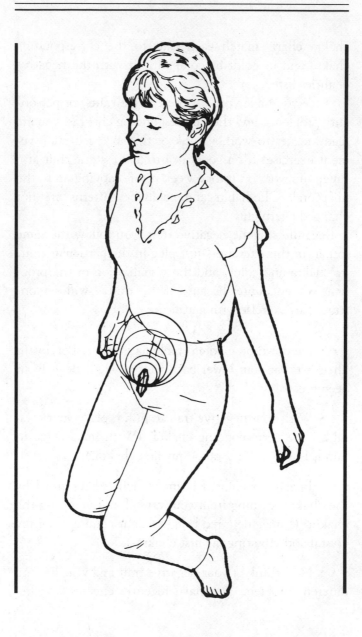

cause of this trait. Remember as many details as you can. (As I focus on my impatience I see myself getting pulled over by a policeman and getting a ticket because of running a red light. Now I feel anxiety—this is the anxiety I have often felt as I waste a day waiting for a phone call I'm expecting or a check that's due. I see myself losing my temper as I impatiently wait for my husband to get dressed for church. I remember a part-time job I once took that was totally inappropriate for me because I was too impatient to wait for a better job. . . .)

• • • Imagine the color vibrating in your chakra and then literally sucking up the negative trait and any problems you recently encountered into your crystal. (I vibrate the color red in my first chakra and see it sucking up all of my impatience, and what I just visualized, into my crystal.)

• • • Affirm that you are releasing the trait as you exhale. Do this seven times. (I release my impatience.)

• • • Remove your crystal from your chakra and affirm seven times: "As light and love flow through me, I am the best person I can be."

• • • Clear your crystal of the negative trait it has just accumulated. Place it under cold running tap water for a minute, as you visualize that trait (my impatience) washing out of your crystal and down the drain.

After you've repeated this exercise daily for a week you will find yourself "on alert," checking to make sure your negative trait is under control as much as possible. When you feel yourself slipping back into your old pattern, begin your deep breathing and affirm its positive opposite. (If I start feeling *impatient* I begin my deep breathing and affirm, "I am patient," as many times as necessary until I actually feel calm and patient.)

This exercise is also a natural confidence builder and does wonders for your self-esteem, as you are affirming, "I am the best person I can be." Since your crystal amplifies the energy you are projecting through your affirmation, you'll find "being the best person I can be" being amplified within yourself.

CURBING YOUR COMPULSIVE BEHAVIOR WITH CRYSTAL POWER

The eighties are a time of awareness, and many of us are constantly reaching for a higher level of consciousness. Besides investigating and hooking up with different spiritual outlets, most of us are attempting to "clean up our acts" by trying to kick our vices and curb our compulsive behaviors, including overeating, drinking, smoking, and drug abuse. The growing number of twelve-step self-help programs that are available indicates how many of us desire personal improvement. Ultimately, what we're trying to do is put the balance back into our lives and to revitalize ourselves after so many years of excess.

Whether you belong to any of the twelve-step self-help programs (Overeaters Anonymous, Alcoholics

Anonymous, Cocaine Anonymous, etc.), or you're trying to do it on your own, your crystal can be a part of your support system to help you curb your compulsive desires.

You can perform this exercise daily, or whenever you "get the urge."

• • • Sit on a chair with your back straight and your feet flat on the floor. Hold your crystal, tip upward, at your third chakra (solar plexus) with the fingertips of both hands. One of the positive qualities of third-chakra energy is *self-discipline*.

• • • Begin your deep breathing. As you center and calm yourself, feel how good it is to have self-control.

• • • As you continue your deep breathing, and feeling good about being in control, visualize your body pulling in yellow light at the third chakra from your crystal. See and feel your body filling up with this yellow light.

• • • Focus on your crystal and as you feel it pulse, know that you are vibrating in harmony with it.

• • • Now begin thinking about the vice, habit, or compulsive urge you wish to eliminate from your life forever. Feel the emotions you associate with it and focus on them. If any visualizations associated with the vice appear, regardless of how unpleasant, focus on them as well.

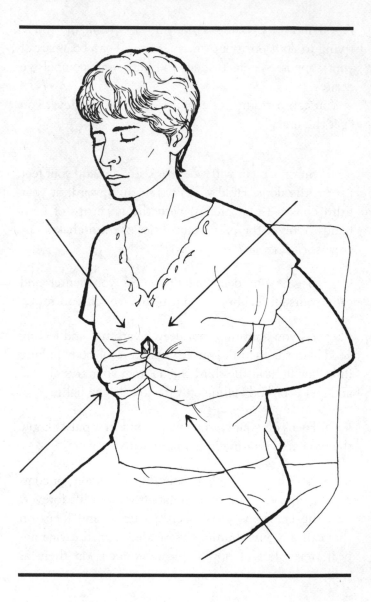

• • • When you have the vice and all the visualizations associated with it clearly focused in your mind, imagine the yellow light being drawn out of your body and into the crystal—drawing the vice and visualizations with it. Think of your crystal as a vacuum cleaner, sucking what you no longer desire to be in your life out of you.

• • • Deeply exhale and affirm: "I control my urges and desires. I am serene." Repeat at least seven times, and as many more times as you feel are helpful.

• • • Clear your crystal of all the negative energy it has just accumulated. Place it under cold running tap water for at least a minute. Visualize the *unwanted* alcohol, drugs, food, or cigarettes washing out of your crystal and down the drain, as you affirm: "I am free of my desires."

While working on curbing your compulsions or kicking your vices, keep your crystal with you at all times. Whenever you get the urge, begin rubbing your crystal in your right hand as you silently affirm over and over again: "I am free of my desires. I send them out into the universe."

Continue the affirmation until the desire or urge passes. Your crystal is an excellent tool for purging your personal "demons."

PROBLEM SOLVING: THE CRYSTAL SOLUTION

One of the most valued skills you can develop with your crystal is problem solving, and it is a skill that improves the more you practice it. In order to solve problems you must be completely in touch with the present moment and your inner voice.

• • • Lie down on a comfortable flat surface with your knees bent and your lower back relaxed.

• • • Place your crystal on your "third eye." Begin your deep breathing and do nothing more until you feel you are in a state of deep relaxation.

• • • When you feel completely relaxed, define clearly to yourself the problem at hand.

• • • Let any pictures or images float freely into your mind. What are you seeing? (Allow ample time before proceeding.)

• • • Listen to your inner voice. What are you hearing? (Allow ample time before proceeding.)

• • • Stay with this meditation for awhile, taking in images, sounds, and any solutions that are making themselves apparent.

• • • Consider all that you see and hear before making any decisions or taking any actions. If your need for a solution isn't urgent, repeat this exercise the following day and compare what you see and hear. Trust your intuition as you follow through with your decision.

So far we have been focusing on your crystal and how it affects you and your inner world. You have learned to use it to enhance and empower your well-being, help you quiet your conflicts, and in general allow you to get in touch with your inner self—your light and your truth. I believe that the ultimate goal for most of us is to be happy, balanced, and productive human beings—to be the best we can be.

But what about your personal relationships? Does the

crystal have the power to make us more diplomatic, can it help us patch up our quarrels, can it save a failing relationship or marriage? Unfortunately there are no quick and easy solutions, but your crystal can vitalize your personal life when *you work with it,* and can help you harmonize your relationships. This means visualizing harmony where there is conflict and affirming "what is" to replace "what really is."

CONFLICTS WITH YOUR LOVER OR SPOUSE

If you haven't been getting along with your lover or spouse, first find a snapshot of the two of you together sharing a loving moment. If you're married, get out the wedding pictures and select your favorite one.

• • • Begin your deep breathing. Hold your crystal in your right hand and as you look at the photograph relax and "breathe in" the happy memories. Remember that happiness you shared; visualize exactly what happened when you fell in love. Try to recapture those intense feelings of love that existed when the relationship first began. In your mind relive all the special moments.

• • • Now begin affirming: "Our love grows stonger every day."

• • • As you continue to affirm, visualize you and your partner loving and embracing one another. See the two of you holding hands, smiling, and laughing as you share a love that grows stronger every day.

Our love grows stronger every day

• • •

If you and your partner begin to quarrel, stop participating and reach for your crystal. Silently affirm: "Our love grows stronger every day" over and over again. You'll be amazed at how the energy suddenly changes from combative to at least neutral, if not loving.

CONFLICTS ON THE JOB

Maintaining harmony on the job isn't always easy because you are a part of many different relationships that operate separately, while they are at the same time parts of the whole. As wounded egos, jealousies, and gossip abound, negativity can take control of your work environment. If these are your working conditions, the best thing that you can do, besides keeping your crystal with you at all times, is to say the Crystal Prayer:

I am surrounded and protected by the white light of
God. I invoke divine light within me. I am a clear
and perfect channel, completing my work
harmoniously. Light is my guide.

I recommend that you hold your crystal in your right hand and repeat this several times to yourself on your way to work. Once you're at your job, know that you are protected from any negativity that is cast your way. Let the rest of them fight, complain, and gossip while you detach from it all and get the job done.

Conflicts with Co-workers

If you're having a direct conflict with a co-worker, and he or she seems unwilling to try to resolve it, the best thing that you can do is to bless him or her with unconditional love.

Holding your crystal in your right hand, affirm: "I have unconditional love for _____." Or, "I unconditionally love _____." Or, "I love _____ unconditionally."

Repeat this affirmation until you really start to believe it and feel it. I realize that this could take days of constant affirming, but it will work. While you may not become the best of friends, your working relationship should improve as you diffuse the hostility with unconditional love.

Dealing with the Boss

Conflicts with your boss can fill you with all kinds of anxiety because you may feel that your job is threatened. If you and your boss are not agreeing on much of anything at the moment, try this simple exercise every morning before you leave for work.

• • • Sit comfortably in a chair and begin your deep breathing.

• • • Hold your crystal in your right hand and place it against your third chakra (solar plexus)—remember that this is the center of your career energy.

• • • As you deeply inhale, imagine that you are pulling in a beam of yellow light from your crystal. Fill yourself with this happy, yellow light.

• • • Visualize the day that you were hired and the excitement you felt. Remember that you have this job because you are capable and talented. Visualize you and your boss shaking hands. Hold this visualization and embellish with details: You are both smiling. You are enjoying a pleasant business lunch together. Hear your boss wish you a good evening as you end your work day.

• • • As you deeply exhale affirm: "This conflict is passing."

• • • Repeat this affirmation each time you deeply exhale. Do this seven times. Now finish by saying, "So it is."

THE POWER OF UNCONDITIONAL LOVE

Regardless of whatever hurt or emotional pain someone may have caused you, when you love unconditionally it usually comes back in a wonderful way. To love unconditionally is to love "no matter what." Your crystal can empower your capacity for unconditional love as it amplifies and transmits your affirmation and its energy out into the universe.

When working with unconditional love affirmations make sure that you are holding your crystal in your right hand, in order to project the energy out into the universe more effectively. As you work with this affirmation, watch the magic happen. It is one of the simplest but most powerful affirmations there is. Regardless of anyone else's actions, when you love unconditionally your relationships will improve.

CRYSTAL QUICKIES, RELAXATION TECHNIQUES, AND PICK-ME-UPS

There are many ways in which your crystal can be used to enhance your life, since your crystal really has as many uses as you can think of. It's up to you, the user, to decide how far to take your crystal power. There are no boundaries or limitations—this is the promise of the crystal. So don't be afraid to be creative.

In this chapter are some of my favorite crystal quickies, relaxation techniques, and pick-me-ups, tried and true. Try them and let them inspire you to go one step further in creating your own.

SOME QUICKIES

You can:

—Bury your crystal in the soil for a day to perk up a potted plant.

—Put your crystal in your fruit or vegetable bin to enhance freshness.

—Energize drinking water by placing your crystal in a clean glass jar filled with distilled water. Leave it in the sunlight from noon until two P.M. Your charged water is ready to drink, filling you with all kinds of insights and energy! (Share some with your pet.)

—Place it on your sixth chakra (above the nose, between the brows) and ask it for the lottery numbers.

—Think of it as your fairy godmother as you talk to it and tell it your hopes, wishes, and aspirations. Follow it up with affirmations, and keep repeating those affirmations several times a day until you get at least one thing that you asked for.

—Put it in your pocket before you go shopping and affirm that you are finding the best dress or suit for you at the best price. I have one friend who did this before going shopping at Macy's. Not only did he end up with a gorgeous new suit for very little money, but a puppy as well. He says he was mysteriously drawn to the pet department—a department he never goes to

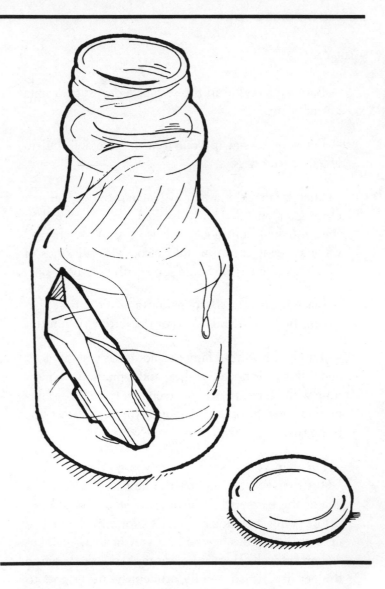

—and there he found a white puppy he couldn't resist. Needless to say, he named the puppy "Crystal."

—Tell your crystal you'll get caught up on your backlog of paperwork by affirming, "I am caught up on my backlog of paperwork." Place it on your pile of papers as you work, and watch yourself zoom through the pile.

—Put your crystal on the dashboard while you're driving and let it guide you to the perfect parking spot. Having it there will also keep you calm while you're on the road.

—Place your crystal on your wallet before you go to sleep. Affirm, "I attract prosperity and abundance into my life."

SOME RELAXATION TECHNIQUES

If you use your crystal for relaxing when physical symptoms are troubling you, it is very important that you cleanse, clear, and recharge it before using it again. For cleansing after a healing, in addition to placing it under running tap water, I recommend a salt bath, which amounts to nothing more than placing your crystal into a cup of salt water for ten minutes before you place it under running tap water. The next chapter will explain this procedure in greater detail.

Relaxation Techniques for Headaches

Technique #1: Here's an easy relaxation technique that can be used while you're watching television, sitting in a movie theater, when you're traveling (provided you're not doing the driving!):

• • • While resting comfortably, sitting or lying down, hold your crystal in your left hand. Relax and center yourself through focused deep breathing. Tune in to the subtle vibrations of your crystal as it lightly pulsates in your palm.

• • • Place your right hand over your forehead. If your headache is at the base of your skull, place your right hand over the back of your head. (Now visualize a beam

of white light traveling up your left arm, through your body, down your right arm, and out your right hand. Imagine it's zapping the painful area, like a powerful laser beam, dissolving the blocked energy that's causing you pain.) As you hold this position for at least fifteen minutes, continue your deep breathing and relax. It's as simple as that!

Technique #2: Try this quick and easy technique for relaxing away a headache during your coffee break, while sitting at your desk:

• • • Sit in your chair with your back straight, your shoes off, and your feet flat on the floor. Place your crystal on top of your head. Now release any tension that you have in your shoulders and relax your arms on your desk.

• • • Close your eyes and begin your deep breathing. As you inhale visualize a golden beam of sunlight shining on your head. See your crystal drawing in this warm, healing, white light.

• • • As you inhale, imagine your head filling with this wonderful white light. As you exhale, affirm with your inner voice: "I release all pain, both real and imagined." Continue affirming for five minutes.

• • • Remove your crystal from the top of your head. Sit quietly for a few minutes, continuing your deep breathing, before you ease back into your work.

• • • Place your crystal on your desk, where it can spar-
kle at you—reminding you that all is well.

Relaxation Techniques for Soothing Tired Eyes

For soothing tired eyes and easing eye strain, crystal
relaxation techniques can help.

• • • Wash your hands.

• • • Rub and activate your crystal with your left hand.

• • • Now cup your left hand and place your crystal
deep within your palm.

• • • Drop your head toward your chest in a relaxed
manner. Close your eyes and place your cupped left hand
over your left eye and cheek. (Your crystal should not
touch your eye.)

• • • Begin your deep breathing. Now visualize a beautiful violet light coming from the crystal, filling your
palm, and bathing your eye. Feel this violet light ease
the strain and relax the eye muscles. Imagine that the
violet light is washing your eye clean of any dust particles
or other impurities. Continue this visualization for a few
minutes until you feel relief.

• • • Now cup your right hand and place your crystal
deep within your palm. Repeat the entire process on
your right eye.

Relaxation Techniques for Congested Sinuses

Whether it's because of pollution, allergies, or the common cold, congested sinuses can cause pain and lead to
infection if they aren't cleared. Here you will use some

acupressure with the energy of your crystal to help release the congestion.

• • • Wash your hands.

• • • Rub and activate your crystal with your left hand.

• • • Rest your left elbow on your desk. Now cup your
left hand and place your crystal deep within your palm.

• • • Close your eyes. Let your head drop onto your
cupped hand, and using the weight of your head, apply
moderate pressure to your cheekbone (directly below the
eye) with the heel of your hand.

• • • Begin your deep breathing, exhaling into the pressure that's being applied to your cheekbone by the heel
of your hand.

• • • Visualize your cupped hand vibrating with white
light. See that vibrating light penetrating your sinuses,
dispersing the congestion so that your sinus is now a
clear tube. Hold this visualization for a few minutes,
continuing to breathe deeply. On each exhalation
through your nose, imagine the feeling of the congestion
dispersing.

• • • Repeat the entire process on your right sinus.

Relaxation Techniques to Help You Rise Above the Aches and Pains of Common Flu

If a bad cold or a case of the flu gets the better of you,
there's not a lot that you can do except let it run its

course. However, with the help of your crystal and some affirming you can transcend your suffering. Regardless of how miserable you feel, try the following exercise while you're in bed:

• • • Begin your deep breathing. If you are heavily congested, it may be difficult to do—but give it your best effort.

• • • Place your crystal on your third chakra (solar plexus). One of the functions of this chakra is the vitalization of your body. Rest your arms comfortably at your side.

• • • As you deeply inhale, draw in through your crystal a beautiful yellow light. As you deeply exhale, imagine that you are expelling all the poisons from your body. Continue doing this for as long as you like, but not to the point of exhaustion.

• • • Finish by slowly, quietly affirming: "I am in perfect health." As you continuously affirm, let it take you into a state of deep relaxation. You may even find yourself falling asleep. When you wake up your body should feel vitalized.

CRYSTAL PICK-ME-UPS

The Quick Focus

When you feel scattered and overwhelmed because of all the different activities in your life, it is easy to lose your

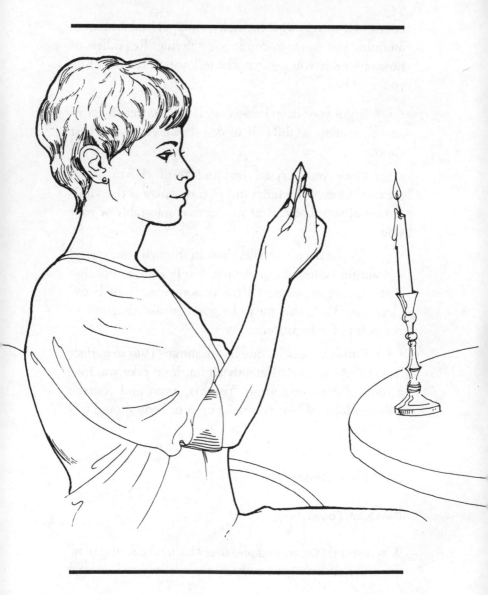

focus. And when you lose your focus, your ability to concentrate usually weakens. Before you know it, you're trying to do everything at once because you are unable to focus on one particular thing. This simple focusing exercise will restore your concentration. Practice it whenever you start feeling scattered.

• • • The ideal setup for this exercise is: Sitting in a comfortable position in front of a table or desk with a burning candle in a dimly lit room. (If you are at the office you can improvise by turning out the lights—except for your desk lamp.)

• • • Sitting comfortably, begin your deep breathing to center yourself. As you deeply inhale, stare into the candle and visualize a bright yellow light entering your body. Continue this visualization until your whole body is filled with a bright, vibrating, yellow light.

• • • Now begin looking into your crystal, as you continue your deep breathing. Explore its inner world. Look for a particular veil, wisp, or inclusion that appeals to you. Once you've found it, study it carefully and see how it looks when you hold it before the candlelight. Now focus on some aspect of its clarity. See and feel your crystal project its clarity and perfection on you. Spend a few minutes with this.

• • • Now affirm: "I am focused. I am clear." Repeat this affirmation at least seven times.

A Crystal Catnap

A crystal catnap taken after work will leave you feeling refreshed, vitalized, and ready to enjoy whatever your evening brings.

• • • Lie down on your bed, with your arms and legs stretched out.

• • • Begin your deep breathing, as you take your body into a state of deep relaxation.

• • • Place your crystal on your third eye.

• • • Continue your deep breathing, as you tune in to the subtle vibrations pulsating on your third eye. Continue to relax and allow yourself to drift into a half sleep.

Most people find that they drift off into a kind of meditative or half sleep for about twenty minutes before they come to. If you're concerned that you'll fall deeply asleep, set your clock radio alarm so that you'll be gently awakened by soothing music.

The Crystal Bath

This is the simplest and best pick-me-up of all, and the perfect way to vitalize yourself after a tedious day.

• • • Put the stopper in your tub and turn on the warm water. The temperature should be somewhere between lukewarm and hot. Place your crystal in the tub while the water is running. Your crystal will be stimulated by the moving water and this will effectively charge the water with the crystal's vibrations.

• • • You can add a small handful of sea salt, herbs, or natural mineral bath preparations (purchased at health food stores, gourmet food shops, and beauty boutiques), but don't add any commercial bath oils or bubbles. Personally, I like my crystal bath with just a handful of sea salt.

• • • Light a candle (to enhance your relaxation) and place it in the corner of the tub, turn off the lights, and get in!

• • • As the warm water begins to relax you, feel crystal energy permeate every part of your body. Watch the candle flame and imagine that you are inside a big, beautiful crystal, being bathed by its healing light—by every color in the spectrum.

• • • First you are bathed in red, then orange, then yellow, then green, then blue, then purple, then white. See yourself being bathed in crystal clear white light. Stay with this visualization for a while.

• • • Now affirm: "The light and the love of the universe flow through me. I radiate my well-being." As you continue to soak, repeat this affirmation over and over again.

• • • Take your crystal in your left hand. Now allow the water to drain as you gradually fill the tub with cool water. As you begin to notice the temperature change, imagine an energy charge going through your body. Stay in the tub until the cool water starts to become uncomfortable.

When you get out of the tub you'll feel relaxed as well as invigorated. And remember to slip your crystal in your pocket or your purse before you step out for the evening.

Throughout the book you have used a very simple system for cleaning, clearing, and charging your crystal. It's the system I prefer because it involves the basics: water, mental energy, and the sun. It also gets the job done in a minimal period of time and with the least amount of fuss.

However, the ritual of crystal care is very important to many people. Some people say it helps them feel more attuned to their crystal and its vibration. Others are convinced that their crystal demands more attention.

And then there are those people who feel that their crystal requires absolutely no special care at all—reasoning that it must be self-clearing and self-cleansing, since it is constantly channeling energy. All it needs is an occasional jolt of sun to stimulate its natural flow of energy.

I believe that since crystals can store energy, they need to be cleansed and cleared at least once a week. For the same reason, they should be cleansed and cleared after any physical, emotional, or spiritual healing.

I suggest that you listen to your crystal, through your inner voice, and let it guide you in its care. As your crystal has many uses, there are many different ways to care for it.

SEA SALT BATHS AND BURIALS

Sea salt is a favorite cleansing agent for many crystal users, and there are many ways to use it. You can:

—add a teaspoon of sea salt to a cup of water and soak your crystal from ten minutes to seven days. (If you prefer to work in large volume, it's a half pound of sea salt to one gallon of water.) Rinse with running tap water.

—or you can bury your crystal in a cup of sea salt for three hours to seven days. Rinse with running tap water.

For a deluxe cleaning, clearing, and supercharge, take your crystal to the ocean and bathe it in fresh saltwater. This is one of my favorite cleansing methods. After I've washed my crystals in the ocean waves, I bury them in the sand next to my towel. By the end of the day, they're supercharged and ready to go to work!

WORKING WITH THE ELEMENTS TO CHARGE YOUR CRYSTAL

Since crystals represent the light, the sun is the perfect charger for your crystal. When your crystal isn't with you, place it where it can catch the light—a windowsill, a porch or terrace.

I have also found that crystals respond well to moonlight, but this may take some experimentation on your part. Remember that the different phases of the moon constantly change the moon's energy. You may want to think twice before you leave your crystal out all night under a full moon.

Like the sand, the soil can also be an effective charger for your crystal. It will respond well to the soil's minerals —just stick it in an outdoor potted plant or in your garden for a few hours or a few days. Make sure that you devise some sort of marker so that your crystal is easily found after it's charged.

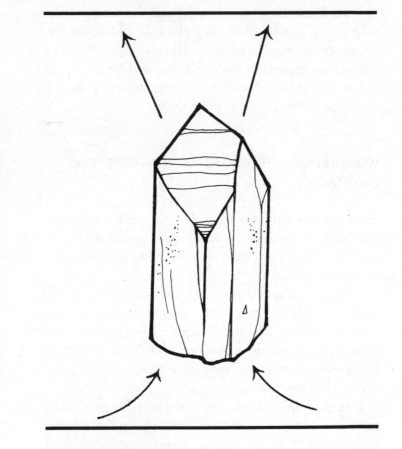

USING VISUALIZATIONS TO CLEAR YOUR CRYSTAL

Clearing your crystal with a visualization after you
cleanse it guarantees that your crystal will be free of any
negative energy. There are any number of visualizations
that you can create, depending on the circumstances.
The only requirement is that your intention be to re-

move any negativity that has accumulated in it. So feel free to structure your visualizations any way you wish.

A standard clearing is to imagine a beam of golden light entering the blunt end of your crystal from the earth. As the golden light flows out of the terminated end it takes with it any residual negativity. Now imagine that negativity turning into light, and send it out into the universe.

CRYSTAL POUCHES AND BAGS

You may want to transport your crystal in a small pouch or bag made of natural materials such as cotton, silk,

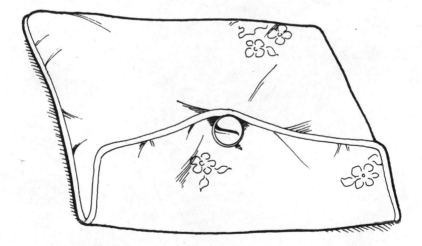

leather, or wool. You can get small silk or cotton pouches from almost any jeweler or in the notions department of your local department store. A small pouch or bag protects your crystal from physical damage (especially if you carry it in a purse), and many users believe that it protects the crystal's energy, keeping its quality intact.

Regardless of the methods of care you decide to use, treat your crystal with love and respect. It is one of the earth's most precious gifts, offered to you for years of enlightenment.

CONCLUSION

If you feel shy about your crystal work, nobody has to know. Your crystal has many uses; it is your personal tool for growth. Don't be surprised if your family, friends, and co-workers begin to notice a "certain something" that's different about you. Remember that the more you work with your crystal, the more vitalized in body, mind, and spirit you'll become. I hope the crystal you received with *Crystal Clear* is the first of many you'll work with in the future.

There is no "end" to your crystal work; only new beginnings. As you go deeper within yourself and your personal potential makes itself known, old hangups, bad habits, and negative thoughts will begin to disappear. As your inner self is illuminated by the light of your crystal, certain truths will be revealed to you, that will make your life and its intentions crystal clear. This is the crystal promise.

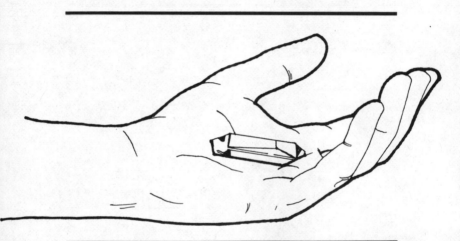

ABOUT THE AUTHOR

CONNIE CHURCH is a free-lance writer. She is the coauthor of *Self-Massage, Powercise: The Elaine Powers Total Workout Guide,* and *Starstyle: An Astrological Guide to Love and Beauty.* Her first book, *Self-Massage,* has been published in nine different languages and is currently in print throughout the world.

In addition, Connie has ghostwritten several celebrity books, including Marisa Berenson's *Dressing Up.* Her articles, covering a wide range of interests including health, beauty, fashion, psychology, and metaphysics, have appeared in national magazines and newspapers across the country.